In Trace Peterson's amazing first book, with its haunted, puzzled, delighted aplomb and its self-wounding, self-delighting nouveau Lacanian calculus, desire is the restless remainder of body subtracted from voice, or maybe it's voice from body. Whitmanian in its quick and tender grandeur, its penchant for direct address, and its abstract kinkiness and longing, *Since I Moved In* moves exorably from the transgendering (non) performance of "Trans Figures" to the started, suspended chiliasm of "Spontaneous Generation," where at last the fetish body, dispersed into landscape, becomes simply an ambient mode of seeing, or saying, in a post-everything ecology where voice broods over the face of the waters, becoming the (prosthetic) body of the world.

—Tenney Nathanson

Since I Moved In is full of undisguised longings that unfold into a larger surface of home, a job, a body, and a life. A texture/al transferring of third person other to a first person subject situated on the thinnest of junctures, where mind meets the gaze. This locus nexus proclaims something a little rougher, a little softer, and something more tender for all of humanity.

—kari edwards

In Trace Peterson's vividly engaging first collection, the voice—voicing—becomes a character that bobs, weaves, tacks, leaps, & refuses to take no for an answer. These gyroscopic acrobatics make the new not an idea but a performance. Peterson's not just moved in, she's made a home for herself on the block and invited us over. Hear, hear!"

—Charles Bernstein

Spinoza said we do not know what the body can do. We also do not know what poetry can do. Trace Peterson's commanding work is all about a new Gaia-like hypothesis: that the body is unity like the earth, and that the strangest seeming perversions are as ordinary as a pet or rat. Transgendered, trans-naturalistic, transcutaneous are all the styles she has on her palette to offer up the "internality of the body," also, the lived and vulnerable prose poetry of entrail and trail. This is Peterson's courageous knife against torpor, dogma, and stupidity. You will be dazzled and perhaps deflowered by this kind of originality and attack's Now you know a little more about what poetry can be.

— David Shapiro

since i moved in

Since I Moved In

Trace Peterson

Introduction by Joy Ladin

The Gil Ott Memorial Book 1
new & revised edition

chax 2019

ISBN 978-1-946104-15-1

Chax Press
1517 N Wilmot Rd no. 264
Tucson Arizona 85712-4410

Chax Press books are supported in part by a fund at the University of Houston-Victoria, and largely by individual donors. Please visit *https://chax.org/membership-support/* if you would like to contribute to our mission to make an impact on the literature and culture of our time.

Acknowledgments: The first edition of *Since I Moved In* was published by Chax Press in 2007. The current edition is significantly revised and expanded, and includes a new Introduction.

Thanks to kari edwards for publishing a section of "Trans Figures" in *Transgender Tapestry* and for publishing "Embarrassment of Riches" in *Transdada*. Thanks to John Ashbery for selecting "Toy" for New England Writers' Robert Penn Warren Award. Thanks to Portable Press at Yo-Yo Labs which published *CUMULUS*, and to Faux Press which published *Trinkets Mashed into a Blender*: selections from these chapbooks appear in the current book. Thanks also to the editors of *Antennae, Colorado Review, Fascicle,* and *Five Fingers Review,* in which some of these poems have appeared. I am grateful to the following readers, without whom this book could not have been possible: Charles Alexander, Charles Borkhuis, James Cook, Barbara Cully, Maria Damon, kari edwards, Jocelyn Emerson, Thomas Fink, Jorie Graham, Carolyn Hembree, Ruth Lepson, Frank Montesonti, Sheila Murphy, Tenney Nathanson, Lin and Richard Peterson, Pat Peterson, David Ray, F.D. Reeve, Matt Rotando, Jesse Seldess, Joel Sloman, and Suzanna Tamminen. Thanks to Joy Ladin for helping me to become myself, thanks to Stephanie Burt for helping me see this book in a new way, and thanks to TC Tolbert, the poets of *Troubling the Line,* and trans and nonbinary writers everywhere for helping make contemporary poetry more vibrant and alive.

Contents

Introduction: Since Trace Moved In

Looking back over the past few decades at the changes in the cultural position of transgender people is like watching a time-lapse video of the rise of a civilization: art, politics, organizations, concepts of identity, time, aesthetics, and social change, have emerged, ramified, and sometimes dissolved with startling speed. That can make it hard to focus on the individuals who have brought all this about. I'm not talking about the few transgender people who have become media celebrities. I mean those whose turns in the mass media spotlight are brief and rare, if they come at all: artists and writers, intellectuals, historians, archivists, organizers of readings, talks, and conferences, networkers and discussion list moderators, founders of magazines, e-zines, and publishing houses, and, of course, teachers whose decisions about what students should read, discuss, and write about daily shape what rising generations notice, value, and consider integral to humanity.

While we can't know now what the future will make of all this is, when historians examine the rise of transgender poetry and poetics, Trace Peterson's multi-faceted contributions should mark her as one of the most important figures.

Those contributions began years before *Since I Moved In*, which won the Gil Ott Award, was first published by Chax in 2007. Back then, there were few collections of poetry that spoke openly of and to transgender experience. This collection announced the arrival of a poet of prodigious and wide-ranging talents, a poet who insisted on planting herself, not despite but because of her gender complexity, squarely at the aesthetic crossroads of twenty-first century

---

1 I use female pronouns throughout to reflect Trace's lifelong female gender identification. Most of the biographical details of Trace Peterson's life were graciously supplied by her in response to my queries.

American poetry. The contested ground this collection claims, the cultural cruxes it straddles, reflect its author's determination to connect, no matter the personal cost, the disconnected social realms in which her identity was rooted: the poetry world, particularly that of post-modernist poetics, which then had little interest in queer or transgender identities, and the world of queer and trans theory, which at that point was just as uninterested in poetry.

When the twenty-first century began, Trace, then still pre-transition and going by the name Tim, was a young poet whose interests, from the first, crossed traditional divides. She studied with poets representing many strains of American poetry, including F.D. Reeve (who had assisted Robert Frost), Barbara Cully, and Jorie Graham, who let Trace sit in on her Harvard workshop. Graham and John Ashbery separately singled out early poems ("Thee and Thou" and "Toy," included in this volume) for recognition. After completing an M.F.A. in poetry at the University of Arizona at Tucson in 2002, Trace became an active member of Boston's poetry scene. In addition to participating in a writing group that included Ruth Lepson, Joel Sloman, Jocelyn Emerson, and Ruth Tobias, she ran a reading series called "The Analogous Series," which featured poets in collaboration with painters, an early example of her commitment to fostering relationships that cut across conventional categories and boundaries. This period also marked the beginning of her career as a publisher and editor; Trace brought out the first issue of the journal *EOAGH* (still going strong) in 2004.

While she was establishing herself as a poet, Trace was also exploring ways to live her transgender identity, making connections in and contributions to a world that most American poets – and, in the early 2000s, most Americans – barely knew existed. After trying and failing to come out as an undergraduate at Wesleyan circa 2000 – no one there understood what she was trying to come out *as* – Trace moved to Tucson to do the aforementioned M.F.A. There, for the first time, she met other transgender people, and found support groups and a community in which trans identities were understood and valued. The combination of the M.F.A. program's demands for poetry production and the discovery of trans community inspired Trace to write many of the poems in this collection that directly address trans experience – and, in the process, to pioneer her distinctive approach to what would later be recognized as trans poetics.

Though Trace became an active participant in Boston's poetry scene after completing her M.F.A., she was unable to find the kind of trans community she had in Tucson. In response, Trace sought connection to transgender community through poetry, an effort that led her to become a driving force in creating cultural space for and recognition of transgender poetry and poetics.

To take one of the most consequential examples, in 2003, Trace initiated a correspondence with pioneering trans poet kari edwards. Though Trace was seeking emotional support from edwards, for the most part, what she received from edwards was poetry: edwards sent her brilliant, often caustic poems about gender, and published a number of Trace's poems, including parts of "Trans Figures," the opening section of this collection. Their relationship continued after Trace left Boston for New York, and grew from exchanges of emails and poems to collaboration on a groundbreaking issue of *EOAGH*, "Queering Language," which Trace envisioned as a means of bridging the gap between experimental poets, who showed little interest in queer identities, and queer thinkers who had shown little interest in poetry. As Trace put it in the issue's editorial statement, the point of the issue was "to find out where a critique of the self and a critique of heteronormativity would dovetail together." Though edwards died suddenly in December 2006, just before the issue was launched, their collaboration continued, as Trace highlighted edwards' work in her own writing and public statements, and edited and published a posthumous volume of edwards' writing, *succubus in my pocket*, which won the first Lambda Literary Award for Transgender Poetry in 2016.

Though "Queering Language" broke important ground, general recognition of queer and trans poets in the poetry world was still many years away. Despite her grief over edwards' death, Trace took two more steps toward that goal in 2007, publishing *Since I Moved In* and embarking on a three-year stint as curator of the Segue Reading Series, which, in her hands, focused mostly on queer poets.

The following year, Trace began a Ph.D. at CUNY Graduate Center, where her studies of trans poetry and poetics were supported financially by the prestigious Robert E. Gilleece Fellowship, and less tangibly but more profoundly by Eve Kosovsky Sedgwick, a mentor with whom Trace formed a close bond in the few months before she died of lung cancer. Sedgwick's death was felt throughout the queer and academic communities; for Trace the loss was deeply personal, coming as it did less than two years after kari edwards' unexpected death. Once again, Trace expressed her grief by carrying on the collaboration death had tried to interrupt, founding, curating and hosting, in Sedgwick's memory, the TENDENCIES: Poetics and Practice speakers' series at the Graduate Center. TENDENCIES inspired and promoted the work of many queer and trans poets, including me. My friendship with Trace began when she invited me to present in the series. When, the night of my presentation, I finally met her in person, she had already changed my relation to trans poetry by suggesting that I write a manifesto on trans poetics, a step I would never have taken without her prompting, and which forced me begin to articulate what I thought trans poetry was and should be.

Over the next several years, Trace worked tirelessly to create cultural space for trans and queer poetry and poetics – and, in the process, kept expanding her portfolio of activities and responsibilities. In addition to TENDENCIES, she ran a poetry reading series at Unnameable Books, a series in contemporary poetics discussion with Vincent Katz at the School of Visual Arts, and an *EOAGH* reading series at Zinc Bar – all while working on her Ph.D.

Trace threw herself into this exhausting schedule as though her life depended on it – which, in many ways, it did. For Trace, the work of creating space for trans poetry was intimately bound up with the work of making space for her own trans identity. Though she was still presenting herself as male in much of her life, she hosted the readings, discussions, and events she organized as herself – as Trace. And so, reading by reading, talk by talk, she was working to create a world in which she could be herself, her whole self, a world in which there was no divide or contradiction between being transgender and being a poet.

Before 2011, most of Trace's efforts to create this world were local, bringing together relatively small groups of people in particular places and specific times. That changed when Trace accepted TC Tolbert's invitation to collaborate on an anthology of trans and genderqueer poetry. Published in 2013 by Nightboat Books, *Troubling the Line: Trans and Genderqueer Poetry and Poetics*, permanently changed the landscape of American poetry. The vitality, variety, and sheer hell-raising excitement of the trans and genderqueer poets and statements of poetics TC and Trace brought together made it impossible for critics, magazines, anthologists, prize committees, fellowship judges, or teachers to pretend that this burgeoning body of poetry did not exist, or that trans and genderqueer poetry was not an integral and important part of twenty-first century American poetry. *Troubling the Line* made it easy for even the most heteronormative gatekeepers to identify and represent trans and genderqueer poets on syllabi, panels, faculties, and tables of contents, in critical roundups and plans for readings.

Troubling the Line marked the poetry-world equivalent of what *Time Magazine*, two years later, would call a "transgender tipping point," a point after which the existence, the presence, the contributions and needs of trans poets could no longer be denied. Since its publication, it has become ever clearer that poetry venues that don't include trans and genderqueer poets have chosen to exclude us.

Not long after *Troubling the Line* came out, Trace reached her own transgender tipping point: she came out as trans, and began living full-time as herself. But as critics of *Time*'s facile formulation have often noted, reaching a tipping point in the awareness of trans people does not mean that others suddenly understand or embrace us. While Trace's poetry world colleagues had become accustomed to seeing her present herself as a woman, they had thought of her not as transgender but as a man doing drag. Many reacted to her transgender identity with amusement, or hostility; some abandoned her completely.

Hurtful as they were, those responses did not slow Trace's efforts to create cultural space for transgender poetry and poetics. Early in 2015, she chaired and presented at a groundbreaking panel on "Transfeminism and Poetics" at the Modern Language Association. Later that year, Trace became the first person to teach a college course devoted to transgender poetry, a breakthrough that drew the attention of PBS Newshour, which recognized that her achievements put her "at the forefront of the push for transgender representation in poetry." The Hunter College class was so successful that Trace has offered it several times, most recently as "Trans and Non-Binary Poetry." She has also taught at Yale, and at Naropa Institute, which has made *Troubling the Line* a required text. In the meantime, Trace has continued her work as publisher and editor, bringing out important collections of poetry by Max Wolf Valerio, Abigail Child, and Andrew Levy, new issues of *EOAGH*, and, with co-editors Gregory Laynor, Eli Goldblatt, and Charles Alexander, the collected poems of Gil Ott, *Arrive on Wave,* published by Chax.

Oh, yes: Trace has done all of this while writing a Ph.D. Dissertation that promises to become a foundational work in what will someday be the history of transgender and nonbinary poetry and poetics.

It is hard to over-estimate how much has changed for trans poets and poetry in the decade since *Since I Moved In* was first published. Though the American poetry world is still disfigured by institutionalized and individual discrimination against people who don't abide by binary definitions of male and female, trans poets are now routinely recognized in awards, anthologies, and magazines; they win prizes and fellowships, are invited to read at poetry festivals, present at writers conferences, and teach workshops and classes. Even presses that are not LGBTQ-identified have begun to publish their collections.

Since I Moved In was written before most of these changes, when few teachers, poets, or readers were aware that there are people who don't fit binary gender categories. That gives the poems that represent trans experience an exciting, improvisatory quality. They have no traditions or forebears to fall back on, no repertoire of moves or conventions to draw on, no way of knowing whether they are succeeding in making trans experience intelligible to those who have not lived it. Each line is charged with the thrill of discovery: not the modernist thrill of making "it," well-worn poetic turf, new, but the thrill of making what had been unspeakable speakable.

But this book is not a historical artifact: it is a moving, wide-ranging, and constantly surprising collection whose subject matter and achievements are not limited to the representation of trans experience. The section entitled "Sites of Likeness" follows Olson and Howe in meditating on the history and remains, physical, social, and moral, of unsung times and places; "Spontaneous Generation" offers lyrical prose-poetic exclamations over various forms of vitality and becoming. Throughout, the poems in *Since I Moved In* display a precocious mastery of post-modernist poetic techniques. There's the reflexive, self-mocking wit, the collaging of echoes from high culture and low, as in "Thee and Thou," which, among other referential feats, mashes up bits of Dante with *Where the Wild Things Are*. There are passages that dance, passages that sing, passages that goof around, passages that sob – and passages that somehow do all those things at once. Many poems skate on the thin ice between sense and non-sense, unspooling sinuous not-quite-sentences that pirhouette and double back on themselves, as in the self-parodic (how could it not be?) "The Age of Advertising," which, after its mocking titular riff on Auden, uncorks vatic utterances like this:

> ... Unless
> greed bend to soda can, gullet meet
> disease for thinking becomes prominent on an order
> unknown to millions of sacrosanct Christian elves
> wearing ear-mufflers.

While it's hard for my heart to go out to those self-muffling elves, in poem after poem, the post-modernist hijinks are accompanied by an elegaic throb, as though their evanescent meanings, however amusing, are spumes emerging from a shadowy sea of loss. There's not a poem in this book that isn't worth reading. Open it anywhere and start reading. You will find yourself in very good hands.

The poems that speak to me most directly are those in the first section, "Trans Figures," which address one of the aspects of transgender experience that I find hardest to articulate or understand: the experience of identifying with a self that doesn't have a body, a liminal self that can neither inhabit nor escape the world of binary gender, a self that is both never and always there. In the untitled, opening poem of this groundbreaking series of depictions, Trace offers a moving, surprisingly simple "trans figure" for this existential oxymoron of a self – that of a disembodied voice:

> The voice wants to turn itself into a body.
> It can't, though it tries hard –

it brings you flowers, to engender a meaningful
relationship. It makes you coffee in the morning.
Here, have a cup.
See, it likes you. It makes your bed
and shows you this mountain vista out the window...

Every time I read these words, I feel a shock of recognition. Though I never conceptualized my own unlived female gender identification as a "voice," I too experienced this identification as something I woke to every morning, something trying "to turn itself into a body" by relating to me even when I couldn't or wouldn't relate to "it." I too experienced its peculiar kindness, the way it cared for the embodied version of me I had never cared for, its insistence on reminding me of the vastness, the beauty, of the world "out the window" of the claustrophic room of my life as a male. As in these poems, it never gave up trying to "engender" – has that verb ever been used more precisely? – a "meaningful relationship" with me, a relationship that would dissolve the dissociation of "it" from "I," of physical existence from being truly alive.

"It" is a terrifying pronoun for many trans people, the most concise and cutting of epithets used to dismiss us. Part of what shocks me in these poems is the ease with which Trace appropriates this pronoun and makes it serve the opposite purpose. Here, "it" is a "trans figure" that makes visible the interiority "it" commonly erases. "It" gives Trace the linguistic purchase necessary to narrate a self that has neither the body nor the history implied by gendered pronouns, a self which, though never "he," has not yet become "she," a self that lives – no one who reads these poems can doubt it – in the subjunctive space between being and wishing to be. These poems make "it" visible without belying its invisibility, limning it against the gender roles it is not tangible enough to inhabit or perform, assigning it verbs that establish it as a subject, inviting all of us, trans or not, to identify with its struggles, fears, disappointments, and moments of hope as it tries to become a body.

Every time I read them, these poems remind me that nothing human is unspeakable: that every experience can be articulated, every perspective represented, and every difference between us, no matter how great, can be bridged by language, which means – isn't this the greatest gift poetry can offer? – that no matter how different we feel, we are not alone.

Joy Ladin
2019

Trans Figures

The voice wants to turn itself into a body.

It can't, though it tries hard —

it brings you flowers, to engender a meaningful

relationship. It makes you coffee in the morning.

Here, have a cup.

See? It likes you. It makes your bed

and shows you this mountain vista out the window

a field of jupiter's beard and beyond it

the dying fields. It shows you things like the sun

going down, and then here it is coming up in the hollyhocks.

Don't look, you'll hurt your eyes. I want

to be there for you, you never respond

in those moments we touch (but they are not enough).

Let me stroke your hair once more, here,

and again here. The voice is growing distant

now, it is fading like the sun fades

and explodes in strands of parti-colored fibers

you will never be able to see.

Let there be breasts! (and there were breasts)
Let there be a penis! (and there was a penis)
or at least it looked like it from the viewer's perspective,
under those clothes. If only it were slim,
with wide hips! (and it was slim with wide hips)
Let there be taffeta, muslin, silk, velvet,
velour, or crinoline: and there were all these things,
in abundance. Let there be hard hats, biceps
bulging out of their shirts, buttocks like boulders
in tight jeans, and there were all these things,
across the landscape. The people looked around
and saw the abundances that language had given them.
The voice envied them. It could have none of this
to keep, but wanted you to think it did.

Smoothed my hand over the plush

Slipping my arms into the sheer

deep sound in my throat

my big breasts filling both my hands

Muscles rippling under my thin cotton shirt

Cleared my throat and began

Trailed blue smoke from my nostrils, like a lazy

Around my shoulders and across

To a party. Forget my hair for now

Clearing my throat, I glanced over

hips were small, and I wondered

Watching my cheeks flex as I suckled

felt hot against my almost naked

Riveted on the full, soft curve

Look around, my gray eyes unreadable

In heels and a skirt, an elegant gesture of the arm

like this, a certain sweep of the neck

into necklace, the voice is trying to manifest

itself. It leaves its apartment after dark,

wondering if its neighbors will see it passing,

crossing the lawn, the tap of its heels

the only sound in the parking lot.

It lives alone. It doesn't want to be seen
by others, but then it wants to be seen.
Sometimes it's driving in a car late at night
through dim streets, fingers nailpolished along
the edge on the wheel, gripping the wheel that
seems bigger this way, seems overwhelming.
The motion of the leg giving the gas
comes from the hip, not the ankle. The voice
is not built like other bodies that do this,
driving around at night. Sometimes it's stopped
at a red light, and the people in the next car
are gaping at it, laughing at its feeble effort
to materialize, some parts in the wrong order, or
proportion. Sometimes the car in the next lane
slows down, because it saw something unusual.
The voice is very conscious of efforts to pass
this trial, tries on gestures that will get it
overlooked, a gentle throwing back of the hair
it saw someone do who was a real body, a bending
forward in the seat so it will seem,
for an instant, like that someone is living in its skin.

Lawn chairs yawn mouth awning

hairs on neck in prayer hands

bandaged ample breast pairs in flown

deck bench stepping stone declension

tensed on step in step represent shipwreck

calling parts dungarees under hands

knees face side of a skin rib filial

injury dingy basement implement tool

swinger pens penis to write and under plans

wrinkled table in full bloom hardy

or wry mouth damaged lock shorn then

The voice tries to hang out with its neighbors, but it's awkward
at this, like everything else.
It hears its own words coming out in a strange way:
"Who's winning? That was a tough play! Oh, man."
Its neighbors Jeff and Tom are accommodating;
they offer it a beer, ask the voice what it's doing
later tonight. It can't tell them it's going
to a *poetry reading,* so it fudges the answer: "Out
to a party or something, probably get real drunk."
It shuffles its shoulders. When it moves from the door
to couchside, it tries to swagger a little,
sits down with one elbow propped on the knee,
leaning in. It takes the beer in its other hand.
The voice detests this ritual, but figures it should
"get out" once in a while, spend time with some people
who don't doubt their status as bodies. They're nice guys,
overall, so it stays in the room and drinks a beer,
talking loudly, throwing its weight around (or what
it thinks might be weight). It doesn't know a thing
about the game, and doesn't care, but joins in
when someone makes a good play and others are shouting.
Commercial time. One of the guys says, "check
out her ass. It's bigger than Minnesota." The voice
decides it's had enough, gets up to leave.
At the door to the dwelling it vanishes.

Don't put on nail polish when you have to drive 120 miles.

Don't wear anything that looks too slutty.

Don't use too many abstractions.

Don't walk anywhere alone late at night.

Don't tell anyone what you're really doing this afternoon.

Don't slouch; walk briskly.

Always buy lipstick that's the right color for your complexion.

Don't get too prosy when you could say it concisely.

Don't let your knees spread open when you're sitting down.

Don't wear anything that makes your shoulders look bigger than your waist.

Don't be redundant.

Don't tell anyone what you're really doing this afternoon.

Always ask the other person about him or her self first.

Don't make gestures that look too 'draggy.'

Don't aspire to be a 'real boy' or a 'real girl.'

Don't use anaphora; it's annoying.

Don't believe him when he says 'I'm laughing with you.'

Don't be intimidated by men with bigger muscles.

Don't begin lines with a preposition.

Don't 'swish around' or 'camp' if you want to be convincing.

Don't censor yourself.

Don't be ashamed of your body.

Don't present your body in a way that makes you ashamed.

Don't wear tank tops if you have a thick neck.

A large thug throws his arm around its waist,

hand clamped over one butt cheek. The voice

shifts a little, to shake him loose

but he grins wider, says "We like to have some fun

around here, no rules." This becomes true

for him, but the voice knows that somehow it's

been shafted. The large thug looks like a gorilla in lipstick.

The voice at this moment is simply a body to be

fucked and thrown away. That grip, no mobility.

Ankle ogle black stocking struck
Match much must

Catch sash ash pretending to wilt
Silt into urn torn

In remnants film or fine pilgrim
Grim nest behave

Have any knee given a film spot
Not down, or strut

But in underneath sundry watch
Mesh haunts

Delirious finger funded injury
Naughty naughty

It lusts after bodies of others, especially yours.
It eyes you as you go to put the milk back in the fridge.
It wants to be close to you. It sits down
here, in the nearest chair at your table.
You know it's a fiction. But at every moment it's
something real, that's its little charm,
collecting the plates after you've finished eating,
scrubbing them. Then it goes out and hits nails
into a board with a hammer. It's very handy
to have a voice around the house. Who says poetry
isn't useful? It can pay your bills, fold them up,
put them in an envelope like this. It can hold you
tight when you need that. It can tell you stories,
like about the time Bob lost his ATM card,
and spent weeks looking for it, thought he had dropped it
in the street, called the police and everything.
And all the while it was right there under the bed in his room!
Bob was a scatterbrained man, but he knew enough
not to give the woman in front of the bank begging
any money, because he'd heard she was the city's
biggest faker, that she went home every night
to a four-bedroom house, and thought about all
those earnest faces handing out bundles of cash.

The deadbeat outside the drugstore was a
childhood friend.

It wanted to go past him and feel up
the packages inside,

the bags of chips, not yet opened, that
crackled

but it tried to pretend there was no story in
the sense of helping

yourself as in 'does it mean to be me'
but his beard was elongated, barbed

but his olive army jacket tore
open at the collar, his face

and therefore the light began to redden
over the prefabricated drugstore roof

but it thought to go inside without speaking
to him the packages, alarming

but the store bell 'dinged' as it passed him on its
way in.

Building blocks: a house, tall with two bedrooms,
a patrician car, a tie, the pet on the leash: imagined,
then real, these things that make it who
and then what?

              Designs for travel, whorl of others,
scenes on the diving board, toenails
painted sometimes, its body starts barging in,
narrowing the options: wide shoulders, lift
them wide, up, chest out: its voice a basso
profundo: jerking gesture, the edge of a collar, square, neck
thick, turning into its opposite, walk from the
shoulders, motions that swing back into the
frame like invisible boxes, close the lid.

Lavender ceilings, professes but in a lavender entrance.
Mottled things at all lavender in lavender.

Correct is to lavender in mottled fingertips as
fingers in caressing at lavender.

> Show at lavender the boys at
> lavender the girls in show

Correct is the girls mottled

> closely is lavender showing?

Is girls lavender at
the lavender closing of mottled
> painting in?

Show my of lavender paper edging out of lavender
mottled face in painting at lavender the girls showing.

It hears a wolf

whistle somewhere

along a leg crossed

over the bench

poses for a picture

but leaps away at

"Looking good, honey"

but the self

consciousness of

moving after being

looked at heard

down from some high

balcony, two men in

baseball caps in

the midst of a beer

sloshing these heels

are killing it, heel

to toe the line of

responding leaving

instead a response

delayed this word and this

is not a portrait of it

Since I Moved In

starting to feel like a real room

or would you say that's traditional

almost typed "toom" then corrected it, Enlightenment

saner and saner, alligator, bars on windows, nut

Orpheus turned around and saw

bungled that too. Orpheus was plugged in

than you. But it seemed that girls were messing things

than your mouth. I wanted

"social change" to attach meanings, although fleeting

ate Popsicles in winter at the pharmacy

were phrases "second pair of eyes," "proactive,"

"on top of things,""move forward with"

"on op of lop top, pings," "funny to be saunas"

you did? I'm finding it harder to continue this conversation since

feet! Why even bother, with all that snow

like technology? Screws up where you get to move

twist and the other up-to-the-minute dances. Gee,

gluttons for techno-enhancement, bud

apotheosis. I'm writing in my pajamas

the interface that has kept me from reaching you.

The Spinal Vocal Animal

Will the left hand and the alien love hand
       still love each other in echo

Fine, you can leave but leaving a part
of saddlebags, marred places on me

Anything in frozen speech moves this limb
       to muse or refusal, alternate feet
broken open, as a tune finds fulfillment
       out of a speaker somewhere. The n'ests
bed down, as the speakers bed down
philanthrophy my right arm gust of wind

     As for imitation,
I see you move in this light which is no light
But synthesized music

             To bear arms, to
discuss the options over imported beer
Steeled teeth against that which is hidden from me

A field, its flowers at my feet,
     Here is an illuminating comment
Were prices rising or falling, your hair dark or
bleached? My hemline rising or falling?

Only pretending
The demolished building falls as the man
        breaks his leg, or the undigested syllable
coughs out a slight indentation. Coat caught.
        Doorways anticipate a thinktank
within reason. Within reason my torso
to be seen or is turning to address your figured glance.

Winter Finds a Ratio to End Itself With

And in that scenario, that tryst, can be found all the policies of the old administration.

Your face, for example, or the check coming back in

and for once the payment was a responsibility one took on.

Tracheas commingle in the morning snow, and the sleds,

enervated but still real, struggle down the hill. Once,

I thought I could be one of a million bodies

throwing themselves out into the open place in the

paths of cars, or hunting at the magazine racks for loose change,

any change, what happens when the next stage of the launch

engages. One minute you were standing on the phone

with a lunchbox and a pile of terrible ideas, and the

next — Whammo! Immersed in a white flight from

somewhere to the future, one eliminated something,

the other numbers, tokening themselves back into the

surface of the calculator's dull face. One drop

was all it took. In the past, I've been obsessed with where

I came from, but never to the extent of snow which

dissolves and melts in the layers of others. Who desires

to fit their career inside the walls of a

canoe, anyhow? The attractive children smile all day, and in the corners

of the room, a terrible lightness settles.

The drink has been swallowed, the angles of your chin half-

shown, but the rest unknown. This is about everything that has no quarter-rest,

no defunct poles or silhouettes, only the harsh language

of the newly set-free miscreants in full throttle over the oars:

the wars had gone nowhere, the wars had gone and none at all.

Correction

But I meant to say that day at the aquarium was a good

day, the gift of her leaning into the Los

Angeles future, heads full of minnows, Don

Rumsfeld cooked up his schemes alongside

The penguin keepers had found companions that

tagged wings, the occasional reef

up to watch the seals get fed

                             Lunch was tilted

into a spittoon of making days want to stand for larger

things, the electric eel (too frightening), room

full of radioactive jellyfish (the picture

intimacy activates false tourist figurine

you took, jellyfish perched on my forehead)

                                 Then we got into

a room where executives were searching each other for

valuables, and a shark's jaw was there you could

touch the teeth, alien to those latitudes

                                 Was that emerging

closer to myself, but bounded by no

memory to staple a potpourri wreath up-

on? The restaurants looked like old wagon wheels, most

at home as tourist of the wild west set, not fitting

into that, bad art in this shop 4th generation Remington

imitators, they have a nicer library here.

                                 Always

bombs were gathering at the base, or mess in words accruing

sometimes too much, as when the Atlantic opens on a

vista, and I catch my first fish but they take it back (too

small), the appropriate English word for spite, squall

tingling like an extinct dinosaur. So this is

what I organize, virtual, out of my virtue!

Minnows, skull still humming from a gift received.

Shadow Lyric

Bare wood turned to a marble colonnade
with a flick of the brush: a balcony,
the stage beyond it. A woman bound
in a boned corset, a forest of "suitors"
somewhere below. A stage —
old stage, a prism like the jewel
that winks a brief glint from another's hand
— and not to say anything at all of the action.
Yes, there was action, but all she saw was shadows:
quick thrusts, a few groans and the fallen,
a few masks taken off (that old stock
comedic device) and an uncle now becomes
a long-lost sister. The soliloquy:
the part where she talks to herself in a room
alone for hours, wallpaper curling
into fierce petals. The view, the ruby sash.
The spyglasses so she can see the expressions
on the actors' faces, though they make their bodies
exaggerate emotion, so that what she sees
is nothing, the distorted close-up focus of
an empty costume, a mask, a little paint
smeared at the edges in the hurry to meet
the cue onstage. The love scene: couples lying
just as we come upon them, in the grove
of innocent confusion, all of those vials

poured into the ear and various orifices,

turning a hate into love, death into life,

a lead that may look like gold but retains

the weight of lead. The balm, the soothing musical

interlude, comes in and she is blessed,

she thinks. This character has walked onstage

now, and she feels that she has known him

all of her life, that she could almost tell him

her most secret thoughts, because of how he cries;

in front of all these people, for no reason

he cries. And she believes him, so she cries?

A Commons

1.

The crabs-in-a-barrel model of artistic involvement
has reached the apex of its use
as an individual winds her clock or esophagus

Guttering syllables, the bereft machine in hindsight
a hydroponic failure, or less. Had a short leash
on that fringe, those friends gathered in surrogate

Plug in! For metal baubles release the hounds' sight
I'm talking about a real degenerate public park, yes
trash strewn around. And someone comes to lift you up

2.

How a commons grows, not a calm rows ascending
influential diadems, nor knocking the heads off
statues. Nor nor, a self-reported sadness

In whose hands delighted the surrogates, storm-and-drain
gatekeepers, pretending to be born? I was
split from the start, warm opposition with

soft hands. The line forms and we join the
pejorocracy, to destroy waking pilgrims
Keep looking forward without ever understanding

Ice cream melts in a float? Felt happiness,
brittle as silk tongs. What was it joined to, what
presence cast a ghostly tongue over that song?

Thee & Thou

An ocean tumbled by with a private boat
buffeted this way and that. As you turned them
over, the leaves were nearly always more or less
wrinkled, and would crumble in your excited hands.
"He was sent to bed without eating" read
another, before it fell apart, the walls in the picture
sometimes very much under cut. Two
circumstances confronted you: you could either reach out
to where he found his supper waiting for him
or close the lid before things got too ugly. Yet
for a freer, more intellectual development
may I remind you that many have gone
without their supper. And the Joe of all
locations, whose kingdom moved forward like a boat
took a more decided turn in the Luxembourg
gardens, where there is no monument to him.
People rolled their terrible eyes and showed
how one could be proud of the ocean kingdom
on the occasion of the marriage of Francesco
to Francesca and still a bit seasick. The water
and the walls became the world all around,
shifting, like when I tell you something
and mean something else entirely. My desires
in metal were brought to a very high state
of finish before the place burned down.

They wore their wolf suits and made mischief of one kind
and I could keep them in without their supper.
The artist was free to mould his design in accordance
with somebody else's eyes, made of jewels.
"Someone has ruined my beautiful cake!" he cried,
and the waves shattered as the jeweled eyes
fell into them. Can you see how over here
this type of doorway can be much better observed
from the other side? You liked the idea of TV.
It said, "Give us all your gold and jewels, and you
shall rule this kingdom everafter." Such doorways
in the country having made their influence felt
in the way one approached that sacred site, the bed.
But look! It was not a real dragon! It was all
a ruse, the reading and the re-reading. See,
in the 13th century, the leaves were nearly always
flimsy like a lie. To the status of gold
they could not get up. The people laughed at them.
The doors swung open and savagely beat
the masonic substructure, but on the contrary,
we picked up fragments of cake that had fallen
over the moat, and galloped into the forest
before anyone could find out we were here
during the period of its supremacy, the book
I mean, whose pages were like some doorway
that tied you up and put you to work making
grape juice. The kaleidoscopic waves

inspired the masters who gave instruction, each
according to his feel for the kingdom's design
(suddenly someone heard a cry for help)

The Age of Advertising

Why are you writing a poem called the Age of Advertising
anyway? What possible ellipses could this metal
plate in my head add to onslaught of capital
credulity? The next fashion arrives. It's dead. The careful minions
wrap my brain in styrofoam. And you, clever dick,
there are so many wars you can attest to out-
side the range of hearing. I need the fad brink.

Hairy though not suffering too much, I take the stand,
turn, counter-stand. I have plastic feet! Why are you
bothering, when it has *so* been done before? Go watch
another no-brow episode in coffers of which the
faint hints of Ajax and OxiClean waft
out of the pale drain from which no available
exit in the last phase of the ancient body shows! Unless
greed bend to soda can, gullet meet
disease for thinking becomes prominent on an order
unknown to millions of sacrosanct Christian elves
wearing ear-mufflers.
                          Well done, the electric hands
shuttle you into the next phase in the boardroom.
I have no aerosol, and the blank stare
envelops me. What makes you so special to the throats
of narcissistic crooning unless time stand
still in the middle of traffic? Cards scattered as the

party in its opulent distinction and the old
performance: little paint, little muskrat tint. If
nothing arises our bohemian conspiring
unravels, shines cruelly.

      There are people watching us
fuck on the dining room table over coffee on
page sixteen although we find it hard to undo
the latches partially the funky decor at the
end of time. Don't you feel the story was
skewed a little in the course of refurbishing?
Black ball and pool cue, furtive place to hide in the
joints. Heaven help your active imago!
Imagine me wearing your socks. I got away with it.

Hemlock

Something's going haywire among the fens;
nettles aping naturalness until they touch you
versus the pretty important password you imbibed:
dark liquid is a good idea. Scratch a late hour,
you replicate yourself in our dark hair attempted access.
Growing out of dirt, like dirt, we archive,
in a central location, the morning's blades. At last
our long grasses pose a security compromise;
rights you relinquish to acquire a strained wisdom
like a post office anesthetized by foppery –
hot cheeks, the fishing emails. I'm sorry,
you've been turned off. The inchworm
crawling up, uh, that thing there in a dark time.
A bunch of malarkey in the weeds wasn't music,
was it? Crossed that line without friends as a scab amends
greased gladiolas, the swan tank full of weeds.
Your ancient seed: we dug it like a house
looks out onto a lake paralyzed
by adept seeing. It grows up around them throats
O pungent carapace, O immersion in that home machine.

A Casualty

Calamity had struck, like the big hand of a clock
or a boxer's rock glove in a face's flesh.

Your table was empty of dishes. The blue silk
curtains dangled in the windows of department

stores downtown. I could tell the ants
carried off some kind of carcass, but I tried

not to look too closely. The languid sand
of beaches stretched out eagerly, and got

swallowed by the sea. These voices filtered
their way through heating ducts and vents

to me. None of us could tell just
how far the brackish underbrush would go,

for those who strode into it. Places were set.
Washing the glasses, scrubbing the surface clean —

that's when the pigeons settled on your rooftop
aerials. I'm sorry the diamond was too big

for its hand. I'm sorry the windows were empty.
I'm sorry that the street was a dry throat, shriveled

like parchment. There was no comfort I could give,
but to say the scene would be full once again

tomorrow with the vendors calling out
the names of their hows and whys. The sky

fell into your cup. There were rings of smoke
and a smell filled the air, as of precious, crushed things.

Light Flooding the Aperture

The gluten days are over, re-patched with a cold stare
corroding the facade of a canvas down to its
blank skivvies. Reality is a terrible thing.
Lewis Hine, why are your factories full of children
closed down, standing in doorways, right arm
missing from where the saw cut it off? Actually,
I find the appropriate place to sit is here. There's
pathos, and then let me tell you what the anchors said.
Who would believe it? As if your eye were a truth,
the cunning of the moment wrapped, pre-shrunk.
I want to step into it and comfort him,
and you, for looking so deep into his face.   Splat!
Another missed angle, and the Eugene Debs cardboard cut-out
falls to the floor in a muddle of his own making, but
warily this time, I trace the lines of your sockets
shine out a worried dream of palatial symmetry, and suffering
makes them more complete than they would be, while you
are lacking in something. The postman comes
today and leaves a paper in a blue bag,
through which I can see the color photo of a
white man in a suit and a Mexican man facing
one another. The time comes to call it labor, the
investment of time. I want to keep you sharing things.
I want to dress your doll in her finery, not those
rumpled dresses, streaked face, unfortunately

frozen in place. I want to direct you to the maker
of the piece, the one whose composition factures,
founders on your runway. The electric day thunders.

My Organelles Monitored as a Single Unit

Under crest or tower, replacing what they speak
with spoken, turn the lid of a jar. Unlike
monkey mind, your arm comes toward my peripheral
field of unfolding, the small of my back
oriented to the sun going down. As robots
crested that wave across crossing out the signs
unfold this way" said Glenda, the packages confirming
as last Sunday the deaf ear rose to meet this
child coming forward, undulant and plain-spoken, "What is the
everywhere, glances off of dualist coffee mug or
concrete (what variety), proprietors fear this spot of rust.

O let them be left, wildness and wet
pitched forth onto a layer of thin green blades
as operational the romantic self splitting
a little afraid of him" but more a salad shooter for
situations elsewhere, at other times, in paint
or intaglio. That's how in the future rust will
bloom, your words coalesce like gnats obscuring streetlamp
strains against plastic cable running down the length of
ambient noise. Those same puritans
pounding hamfisted on the doors again, after the game.

The house I retire to has lyric but no private words
as an oxygen molecule breathed by a founding figure moves through

figure of desire replaced by hierarchical

minibike or weed-wacker. What then, box hedge, what

then, new car smell? Funeral attendants

move homeward, in looking toward this overturning. People

who can trust the state and digest euphemism?

Blood rushing through vesicles, they apprehend the rust,

which is part of me. The fir on the corner, the curl

of the crest in bone, or sound of the uncut

grass. Who refuses to mow that.

Song

Several claims vied for our attention:
loneliness was one. Then there were those thoughts

I could never admit to. Another was a timely
film which settled over the mirror

when I took a shower. And often time's current
nearly pulled the jukebox cord from the wall.

Joints pumped loud, but hands could tear them down,
individual hands, picked out in the light

of stadiums, or clubs. Verses sprung
up on both sides of the path like dahlias, all

the while crying, we have the cruel antagonists
of feet. You wondered how high the apartment

building went. There were so many questions.
We were kept in the waiting room to figure out what happened.

Why were the boots in the hall so gargantuan?
Why, if we slept all night in the camper,

did the rain fall and the globe continue
turning and the jacuzzi bubbling and the

Army fatiguing? How could this be true,
I asked myself, so many roads leading to

the same black box? And now I ask you.
Product is the attraction. One might become

anyone's beloved, and vice versa. This is quite
a dance, you and I, us and them. Yet

the moment I say this, love, I will not have
considered what snow is, what rooms we move through, or how

those asterisks on the page's periphery
still lead to some other, alien geography.

Impetus

I could see you sitting in a library somewhere

laid back like this, one hand up on a statue.

Why would your mouth be that shape, I'd wonder.

Why would the ceiling show cracks, your dusty albums

piled in a corner? Admiring looks

will come, the splashing of mercurial designs

in through the skylight. I would be there too,

in time. Your portrait shines at the end of a hall.

I'd think of this time as razors skim

across a skin of barbasol, leaving all

spotless. I would tip the scales till they flashed

their signal. Then, one hopes, the snapshots

of shaky hands would come into focus, or dimes

would finally get picked up from the road

and put in protective coverings. Everyone

would stand in the entrance hall, waiting to hang

umbrellas in any closet they could find.

Everyone would hear you for miles around

like I do. That the boat might plow through water,

and we, anonymous passengers, feel the spray.

Toy

Darling, come here. I need to show you some
new gadget that will change your life, and give
you hours of enjoyment. Press that button there,
turning the pattern inside-out before
you get too bored to give a damn about
what will happen next. Trust me here,
if you are titillated by the sight
of prison bars, then I am too. I guess
we're stuck together, me and you. Doesn't
it look like we could not be torn apart
unless someone took a saw and lopped off
my reasons for waiting in this corridor,
shifting from foot to foot, like a windup
gadget that dances grotesquely when you turn
on the jukebox? People stampede just
to be the first in line to press your buttons.
Me, I would rather take it in my hand,
the pattern, before something disastrous
happens. You & friends will come home from bars,
exclaiming just a little too roughly, how
cold it is, and how it made your day
just to see a woman smile across
the room at you, before she brought her hand
up with the pert middle finger extended.

The Pleasure of Arriving

Familiar yet strange. That's how I felt about
so many things in those days. The teetering
grapevines hung down over your head.
Everything went as expected. The tongs
bit down on the thing grasped, the nutcracker
dug into the nut's flesh, the thinktank people
hit the nail on the head. Even then.

Call me ridiculous, but I know that wherever
vellum can be found, one also finds magnesium.
Rolling along on backstreets, the pirates
were sighing with so much work to be done,
gallantly, in true pirate-style. The pages were
cut in just the right places to be charming, a scrap
jutted picturesquely out of the sideboard like
effervescent music overflowing its boundaries,
yearning for its big break.
                              The clock says
the idea of sleep will cause a revolution
right at the turn of the second hand into night.
Everyone will be stoical about it. Clocks,
never appreciated, will hang limply over
any objects nearby. It will be a feat
just to remember what you did this morning.

Yes. I'm sorry. Is that correct? My hands
will grow to the size of cubicles and then
badly critical of what you had to say, I shall rise
with kinetic vigor I shall leave the table where
uncovered innards of the last knowledge could
be found largely inadequate. I wonder about.
I wonder. That's a fine hat, the one with the mounted
effigy of our own mayor, that outlandish
effervescent behavior of the dials and groves,
grasping the light and being just a little too forward.

Regulation has its purpose. I hate the clock,
dragging up these old injuries, as in a skating rink
unfortunately, where teetering couples whoosh by
completely engrossed in the act itself. And may
usurpation be the only stoical selection
in the vending machine? Say no more,
for when we see the innards you shall know a
great deal more than you do now. One hates
showing pirates how this process works, yet
how else can we form these alliances? A scrap
gets things going for a while, but doesn't last.

Even the boundaries were drawn up temporarily.

Good news: the one who bathed you as a child
tells me that the Nutcracker plays in the theater
just now, and then again, and then
unendingly like a vending machine that spits

volumes of garbled tickertape out. And so
very good as our synopsis may be, the grooves
on the record may be different the next spin round.

Sites of Likeness

Kelsey

A farm in Saratoga New York 1775 — My ancestor Joseph Kelsey milking cows in the barn — outskirts of settlement pending war — "Tories dressed as Indians" came up behind him — tore the skin from his head scalp torn — public guilt but a private innocence arbitrary — collapsed in the stall — inside the "Indians" found his wife baking bread — hung her from rafters by hair of head — chased down his son nailed his palms to the floor.

Yeast kept rising in bowl on the table — word salvage tendrils implied public body — overflowed covered the surface — we were in said group we believed said thing — a price on his head — Saratoga a native word adapted — did not intend to — Wife freed herself got the boy loose — fled to their father's house with silverware a teakettle.

Hartford: Hooker's Statue Dwarfed by the Skyscraper

William Kelsey, in a group of ten, founded the site for Hartford, Connecticut in winter to prepare it before Thomas Hooker, the "real" founder, arrived the next spring. The way history goes he might as well have put down his flag and made a statue of himself outside the capitol. The view from here, Kelsey's memorial stands in a cemetery down the street around the corner from a giant gold-plated office building, cast shadow. Kelsey was my multiple-greats grandfather and came over on a ship with the "Hooker who founded Hartford" (now on t-shirts, bumper stickers, pencils). Once Robert Lowell wrote a poem called "Christmas Eve Under Hooker's Statue" it was big in its day we shall not be concerned with that here. Several times I passed beneath this statue of some colonial man and there were gangs such as the Latin Kings. Could be dangerous to walk south to where the poorer neighborhood sprung up through sidewalk cracks. Could be dangerous to walk past the gold-plated office building beneath that shadow, past the graveyard where one found Kelsey's memorial to, within a few blocks, housing for the poor.

These contradictions to be aimed at in a parcel. On the one hand, the enormous crystals of capital, glittering obscenely. On the other, the archives, her knowledge that what ascends will pass the gloss of past landscape onto present. The fetish of objects in a glass case, play of light changing across the face of the monument. But a spread of root systems underneath — unearth any sediment, excavate loss like this.

The Gauntlet

The high school wants to be seen into. Yet its shell, a square concrete structure, could be a prison or containment unit. This reinforces the stories we have heard we shall not discuss it further.

Many conjectures, this house placed next to that, trope of tour guide. The campus of Trinity College, founded in 1823, ran a fence around its edge to mark boundaries. One approached the main gate via a row of ramshackle houses boards falling off them. Windowpanes missing also roof tiles. Inhabitants stared from porches, out of work a family? Scrutinizing gauntlet for the scholar of Trinity College, the scholar most likely who was passing and felt a twinge in the center back of the skull. Hands steering in the silence. The falling-apart houses were imagistic the picturesque gaze came barging in. The Main Street buildings were studio apartments used to be old factories. Highways wound around these husks on their way to the downtown and past a skyscraper where one might picture Wallace Stevens working at his desk in an insurance company, Aetna subdivision, aspiring to a silence outside the life below. If money can truly be called a kind of poetry, around the corner the Oasis Diner used to serve good food but now is under new management. Could be dangerous not to mention the soup kitchen in a church basement on Asylum Street, where a man lamented this state, a server held aloft a spoonful of food. Trinity College pays no taxes it looms at the end of this corridor of houses.

Spingarn

Downstreet from Bogardus Hall Leedsville— mansion surrounded by stone
walls — Joel Spingarn and Amy Spingarn — "Troutbeck" named it after the
Lake District England — transference we put down said town here — named it
after said place of origin New — Spingarns built own house stone from the site
field — now a conference center for corporations — library remains but many
books replaced.

Founders of NAACP — patrons of Langston Hughes — story repeated each
time driving by — as if we could forget — and not just because they —because
we knew them —you could have met him just imagine.

Amy Spingarm dropping off a gift for my parents' wedding in Sharon —
flowing black cape driven there — unwrap an ivory cupid — mantle in the
house these objects.

Excavating the Green

At the far end of Asylum Street, Bushnell Park. The first one of its kind pastoral refuge, before the Emerald Necklace, before New York's Central Park. The green expanse I often walked and its sterility a few trees the new capitol at the peak of its hill glinting ambiguously.

Under the green expanse though invisible a swathe of filth, muddy street cobbles, a brown mill river. The houses of poor residents leveled to build a stage for grazing. Families evicted to "improve traffic flow." Participles accomplished it's too late now.

Horace Bushnell introducing the park to the board: "where high and low, rich and poor will exchange looks and make acquaintance through the eyes; an outdoor parlor, opened for the cultivation of good manners and right social feeling."*

Homes turned inside out, spilling onto the green pastoral carpet. You wouldn't want to go there now it's too dangerous.

If you see a man walking toward you across the park from a distance, not following the paths but treading on the green, carrying a sack or backpack, a man made dark by the sun setting, a man waving as if he knows you, though the sun is going down behind him, run.

* Domesticating the Street: The Reform of Public Space in Hartford, 1850-1930. By Peter C. Baldwin (Columbus: Ohio State University Press, 1999)

The Commute

This house in Glastonbury Connecticut, maybe a
little haunted, later to emerge as a residential suburb for Hartford.

No one lived and worked in the city both. Neighbors sold insurance at
Aetna or other companies commute suburb as garden-city ideal urban and rural.

On the way home from work one passed the dome of the Colt factory
painted blue with stars and capped with a gold ball a Russian imitation.
      Churchgoers their exotic firearms.

Neighborhood very green but a few lawns overgrown.
Up in the hills richer section houses gave way to fortresses.

Downtown over here, a string of restaurants and lights, potpourri stores.
Beyond, huge marshmallow-colored buildings a new mall was under construction.

Houses creaked. Potpourri wreaths on doors belied the drugs at parties
held in New England woodframe structures with white clapboards.

A quiet here on the town green, placed next to the graveyard. A gravel road
divided them. One ate hot dogs at a festival the dead always in one's line of sight.

Mumford

Border between Sharon and Amenia — Lewis Mumford the writer and cultural critic lived/worked — my grandmother's family knew him in what capacity — unsure because of urge to orient oneself — association with famous people — we knew *said* people we were doing *said* mundane thing — we knew where we were when Kennedy died — the strange brooms and knikknaks in the corners of the house they all come from somewhere — we can tell you come closer.

My mother's visits to Mumford — grandmother: "why don't you...?" — talks in his study — authors Arnoldian culture cultivation wild garden — potential quotes for books hung — notecards on a string above desk — quantifiable discrete units — held up by clothespins aired out — inscribed a book to her *Sticks and Stones*

Wherever these villages were well-established, they kept sweet and sound over the centuries: in Connecticut, Sharon and Litchfield and Old Lyme...some of their essential form will underlie every sound modern plan for a life that brings together rural and urban functions, not to say felicities.

He complained of the sound of lawn-mowing — had sprung up on weekends a drone — when is hard to say he refused to mow his lawn — he told my mother and instead he let grass and flowers grow waist high — cut little paths through it liked the wildness in his yard.

Malls Move In

At the Christmas ornament shop *I feel like a peon*

chic houses painted with trim it's safe to go down

the sidewalk the cars chuffing along slow-paced

except when she saw the naked man waving at her

from the woods the nature preserved apple cider hay

rides deliver me from Satan as we turn the corner the

bales shift at the office building desk *I feel like a peon*

cars shine in tranquil amusement of emergency

him? *Sure, I know the old man* then malls

move in, the scaffoldings sprout imported weed

should be glad exposure to the outside

network less provincial summer jobs *you can't say*

their name, or they'll come and get you indicating

retreat from the violence next door breeding

wariness toward the skinhead boy down the street

is moral home where the curtains remind you

of nothing we care about this community

that's why we're keeping your taxes low next year

out on the soccer field *I feel like a peon*

this food is delicious *no broken glass in it.*

Middletown

Founded in 1650. Later Samuel Russell brought in money earned from the Chinese opium trade in the 1820s. Ornamental buildings on the Main Street of Middletown crested with decoration thriving port on the river.

Samuel Russell's house, which he made into the image of a Greek temple, complete with entablature, belong to the university that sits on top of the hill. Its pillars are made from New England wood, painted to look like marble.

The map: A main stretch of town ran parallel to the Connecticut River. Railroad tracks leaped over the water going somewhere more important. Bottom of hill, the obligatory Main Street from which capillary outlets flow. Bank buildings, fronts on stores aspiring to be someplace different.

Next to the university and slightly down the hill the housing projects. Gauntlet leading to open green college buildings beyond it. Many times I walked the approach up this hill and the same twinge. Children playing in a fenced-in area covered with soil. Their parents leaning on the fence.

Drive-by shootings in the north end down the street. The bartender there kept a loaded pistol in his apron.

Could have come upon a statue by the river, I guess it's supposed to be of Columbus, off to the side in a sterile little park. In line with this, an Italian restaurant and entablatured building: "Garibaldi." The eyeglass store with its official seal in the window: "Endorsed by the Italian Community of Middletown."

No one visits the town green anonymous statues the map is not the map.

Sharon

Our own tradition of city building includes the New England village which was indeed originally an informal kind of Garden City.

— Lewis Mumford

a town green founded 1739 *I am the Rose of Sharon and the Lily of the Valley*

view of trees in fall a wind scope houses in a line no stores or malls

quiet one hear the branches rustle barely an empty square some roads

dirt time forgot gently simmer wind from below gentrify a lane family

dress moment swing a right here fields open fields what connects

everyone knows knows everyone suffocate shale close door lean

against neither poor nor rich stillness most farmland gradually

houses cover closeness to field a church landscape dotted

own a land gauge language fronds a ghost script sigh

from acre come inherit place shore up steeple

you we are pointing at yes you speak

tongues a congregation

share stillness

Desert Litany

1

Error tourist: thinking that when I come into the city through its dust which is the absence of formal gates, I judge it. This wall here, this house, clay, adobe or fake fiberglass, this man with a golf club following me out of the convenience store waving it over the trunk of my car, dust in one's eyes, this woman here, flipflops a shoulder bag and cell phone, these husky men in a pickup shouting threats at the last red light, all of us sliding past each other, past, enables me to slide by without contact in each case, no people but behind walls of sealed-in glass or dust into eyes as head turns: *You must be from the east coast.*

2

There are no towns as such: there is one city rising up dressed in its own lights.
To think all around its liminal area a desert stretches stresses the freeways, cars
in lines grinding their engines. Building out into the landscape — not up, out.
At the bank, a woman in line to her daughter: *Everything goes real fast where he
comes from. Then they move out here and get a surprise.* She has *no teeth,* in the
mouth, transitional spaces, to find it: *hang a left at the Staples.* The disgust of
that, past a few dusty adobe churches, Christian vanishing point. I judge it, the
refugees dying for lack of water while crossing, the stretch of strip malls here
dismal planning, the traffic jams, homeless man staggering over as I step into the
car, presses a face against the window.

3

Judgment and ferment: back home, people don't conjure up this coast mentally, any of its water or cactuses. Physical world firmly in front of them, *no we know what you're like over there in the west.* Meant nothing by it, of course, bringing out the wine-in-a-box for guests, no one lingering on the subject at parties. At every store I bear the stamp of this inability to eat dust and like it. Secret language, however it may materialize in drive-ins and everything accessible by car, road sprawl — weeds overgrowing these communities. The wheel, govern the road, the will, budge the cargo, spin, over the earth no touch, judge me for this, the inability to be where I am.

Bricky

So now I've escaped to a debonair encampment. Less hungry than meal-jealous, I've come around flocks of hoodlums and bearing-down. Broadway is a kind street lifting glad notion of what we make possible: I planted that median in the center with grass for you. Automatic sprinkler. Being too dangerous to indulge my bodied presence, I have to skirt and peck around the edges of monuments. That's ok, the way we always corrected it, shifting one leg on the bus toward the truss. Families and unlived organs inside me, I'm parading hands over every- thing one sees but can't reach. I'm a little disgruntled with a coffee in one hand and an over- wrought leer. I'm Cambridge one moment, then I'm not. We could throw around zip codes and define our territories: here, you try it. I have taken your zip code which was in the poem, and which you were probably proud to have stored up all winter against the effete opponents of that new legislation. The rise of the anarchists in June blooms! Like a limpet held to a rock, I stay to what moves me, though it curves around in dramatic curlicues and subur- ban you-don't-give-a-shit. A man walked across the bridge, and picked up my dropped pen. It becomes too gaunt a reprisal to live within. To thank the owners of real-estate in their teal buildings downtown — I'm running out of apathy. Protagonists are unlike phantom bellydancers, I think we've established that. Teach me about lust and what repeats I've missed. Calm me down earlier than stores close in Cambridge- town. Buttoned-up and stealing away, you think it's "our thing." The lights collide in the distant town for you. Oh, the cornices organize to bring down structures in your honor.

Your Material

There's a lot of taffy to worry about when making art is the same as not making it. Between my teeth, there, the whole spell undoing your pajamas I found the old role scintillating. It was me, waking up in a room someone else wallpapered, saying over to myself "the record of revolutions" and evolution, catching up to the present. There's a lot to worry about when my hands are less useful than a syringe. Let me get that for you. I throw this trash in your way because I want something unexpected and beautiful to happen between us, like a pair of enormous red lips sucking down a malted trope. There's a lot to worry about no clothing free of identity, no identity free of clothing. I put on a slinky black dress and straddle you, or in the morning I digress a little on the subject of pancakes, blueberry you recede and therefore dilated, enlarging as I hold up this magnifier: there's a lot to worry about when planar stations on Mars have taken up residence in your sad eyes and shoelaces. There's a willing participant. There's a lot of garbage lying around in space: bottle caps, tin cans, detritus of fast food joints, cigarette butts, napkins, someone's flannel nightshirt. Hey someone, here's the last pomegranate of the season. Don't forego it.

Embarrassment of Riches

The grotesque imbalance of powers fuels my morning walk: azaleas, blue phlox, curbside junk. The careers of several generals winding up in the "cult status" bin, partially on account of the long night and a Lexus SUV. Part the mysterious foliage of a potted plant in the company hallway.

No harbingers, no gusts of atrocious statement. We are a free country, and in that dialysis we derive our nutrients from unfair advantage, not unlike arm-wrestling in gale-force winds. The occult language denied to me by my ancestry will emerge in news photos of the battered and the dead.

Fringe benefits. Cola. I had to try on an appearance I wore in the recesses of a dream. In the dream there was a private anchor, and I sat on top of it and rode it out of the water onto the boat. The vessel of our sleeping company lurches forward, flank or wing.

The people around you, brain-dead though they find their polls, learn you a thing or two. In practice, the arms of the republic should embrace those who differ in hair color, build, or perception. A sequined dress, barren angle in the new world, apotheosis of corona and self-stink.

Wink. The news carried us into the souped-up sand dunes. Partially, I grow nostalgic for the intimacy of a nape, but this timidity runs fallow under rifles and manpower. I did not side with the victors. I did not lose my change on the wrong bet, rusted machines of the hard-of-hearing government.

Popular Fronts

You're the top, you're a pillar of the community, you're the top, you're faking it along the way, throwing it together. You're inching forward on a plank two inches wide over a pit of snarling gators, slightly perturbed but shot through with spotlights from the big top you're the gators in the pit, tough hide hid scars, you are many and the spines on your back your long stubby tail you're the top, you're the Louvre Museum you're the Tower of London you're Nelson on the top of Trafalgar square Trajan's column you're the painted woman, Roman, on the wall of a villa, you're the mother who brings her kids lemonade and a little plate of chocolate-chip cookies, you're the top, you're diet cola you're the magazine racks at the store, multiple but unified in a general drone, highly-colored, containing unusual advertisements and distracting me from what I was saying multiple, changeable top you're the child spinning in the yard, plaintively living out the hours in a reddening day you're Garbo's salary you're a stingray you're diagonally stretched by the power grid, now in focus, now distorted I like you that way the tap-dancing monkey on the street, the angel-hair pasta on my dinner plate.

Spontaneous Generation

It starts with a flow, under which wild plants grow, in the current, the opposite of death. Become hands, reaching upward, out into forearms. Tangible aesthetic summer, underground torso coming out of it.

*

View one: the eye that emerges from that water. View two: from the eye's perspective, a landscape. Not pure or signified, pasture or pastoral. Not a thing of beauty, a polluted stream. That life could come out of it nothing short of a miracle, joined at the waist with that other notion, progress. Hoping something mutant but vibrant and a live feed.

View three: the incorporated body. Crowd of these rising out of water in a birth, skins coated with the slime of the dead earth.

*

They are not real, any of them, but they're me. This one has my eye, that one my admiration, that one taking up my gesture in a ruse of its skin. Hardly unanimous, but I can be a part of them, all that I see, same air permeating us, touch and be touched as a word to its hurt thing.

*

A patch of skin is a color against a background rising. Dark, slut, camphor, duct tape summer. Animated sloth of carpal system, dole. Apart from that, lurking in the waste that feels earthen, pretends to be that thing as mall lights simulate fire, to fireflies, to fading stars.

*

The creek breeds life out of death; predilection, orange peels, the remains of housecalls, holding out lungs to breathe with, fiber-optic eyes to see. It feels ashamed of you & not your reflection.

Poor philosopher, poking in the dead stream with a twig. You have been projected behind yourself on a screen. Your reflection stymies all efforts at recognition. They see this part of you, machine. Not flesh, not what you tried to do.

*

The other side of that is bright. Body of light, of solidity and change.

These parts of me I cannot deny: the space I sit in, the left arm muscle moving into the neck causing headache, colophon of sorrow from another time. Made manifest, a bulb opens in the street.

*

I heart the bright office with pants on and a roiling stream of people moving through it. Confined to me by my papers, rent and its functions of living seem normal. Firm black line on a sheet of acetate. I heart my bee balm in the window, my bourgeois rings.

Nothing pilfered, nothing gained. Stagnant, almost. Though I move through space with shopping bags, the strain animates them. Makeup cracking as it fails to fit the mouth beneath it.

*

But delightful! The animating system, checked-in, heart-to-facetime continuum, I pass them! Ordinary folk among green plants, plastic, or fans of that band! We need facilities, we need our desired cables and their message streams.

*

We talk and it simulates origins. You came from a state somewhere outside my periphery. I, opening an orange soda, become my trade. Ordinary man, with a woman's hands.

Across the street, mirror-flash in the window lends both nostalgia and hope to the aesthete. Reprimanded subject, you hope to be in pictures, to be "some body" someday.

*

It happened to them. The containers, the ornaments happened to them. They become, in time, a kind of dependence on the background changing, like me. My hand lifting a soda, changing like me and changing. Blood running through my veins that you oversee.

*

As when I say sight is a terrible thing, I mean sight is a terrible thing. Thus water-filters hide the real toxins and detritus.

You bet your ass. On display here in the party, part that lifts, I adjust my skirt slightly and splay myself against this wall, seductive. J covers his eyes then, as anyone would.

*

For my illuminated public, tension between throat and parlor-trick. Not choice, like running into a wall, bruise wells up, continues welling and you get up and slam into it, again.

*

At the party, one overhears these conversations: "I miss it when they used to give horse carriage rides in the park." Or alternately, "We must now look forward only to a phosphate tongue, a metal skin."

Neither seems appropriate. The caring angel, too passively concerned, or genial ("storm rolling in"). The other one (he's tattooed) too blithely optimistic, as if war was not the root of forgetting, or inequality the sun memory set in.

*

To conclude that they will find a way to use avant against us, aghast, too pessimistic. Everything too too, like your hair falls in ribbons and the anchored seam of plants moves me deeply. Too airy for this world, too unable to speak its name.

Flings with language only relevant beside pace of my own Adam, its stretch or build, its alarming notice. When I wake, each morning it finds purchase in the things around it, word choice, apostrophes, the whole gamut.

*

Oh chair curtain sun the delivery van and the street, rides fate. Oh stares, practical shoes, rooftops, noon.

Oh stolen tune.

*

The inside of my neck would scare you, in all seriousness. It's enormous, contains organs I never could have known would exist: a piano, thunk, or a grandfather clock.

*

Let's take a look inside it. To have never seen down there, aside from a uvula dangling, spurs further curiosity about what caused that bulge then. Adam bites fruit, ripe foot from root word is his skill, or skull. I conjure up a whole school from fruits and football.

*

When a sound begins, it lurks down in trenchant, rolls up into a vibration, then a roar. Throat clench, soft palette lifts. Can't hide from us, Adam with a clenched fist, unconscious.

The bulge, vibrating as the bugle is to call dawn. The veil lifts, this girl has two chins, churlish grin.

*

Over there, that's the end of the tongue. Giveaway as how I heroically put myself down. Dismissal of pleasure, and of being in the moment, growl growing beneath the public role.

*

Not hearing alone, something close to me as my inner organs. Throat wants to be what it echoes, bat sonar, a stone's throw.

Entering a dark room, edge of the corridor. Edge of the table, of the nightshade and the bed. Edge of the dull shapes, so you speak and the trough fills with experience, monad. Honors and trophies, glass, carved figure, an unopened flask.

*

A hostile, ridiculing muse came to me. Was the modern muse, assembled from bric-a-brac. It had the wrists of a painter, the arms of a famous statue, a car's chassis in place of a torso, square.

"The boheme is dead," it called from within its Bob Ross head. "Why ornament, or try? I found some delectables on a tray."

*

I flew in the face of that incorporated waste-voice, felt it was maybe goading me to act as well. A first important step was to inhale the air, along with its smog and haste.

No more, the delight I found was seemingly endless, in fields of nomenclature and political collapse just about to occur. What's behind the microphone bare, but you could sit there.

*

The amaryllis was coming out on the avenue, I knew. Though no one could see the traces of that yet. Though no one could understand what those words meant, they sounded good, they swayed to that sheen.

*

In Chinatown in Boston, I am eyes missing the bank machine, teller replaced by toll, replaced in turn by rack of magazines. I am bad potato chips, a finder's fee.

*

I hurt, hold court, animosity rising over fresh vegetables laid out under misting of steam.

I am each eye in the crowd as the actor rises, screams, an insect's hell among folios, heartless articles.

*

There was one rung, this rung, on the ladder meant I could reach it. Edge meant, nonchalant. There was oaken promise in a fleet of boats blessed by beribboned men, officials, breaking bottles across their decks in midstream.

I tried to reach it. I was April and the funds that created it. I was inside the nose that took in that ancient odor's nomenclature.

*

Breeze, and then they could find it. In a cold room, I was a body beneath the megaphone, body under a sheet, chalk outline drawn around it.

I was pulled outside my own outline by anonymous hands.

*

Outline, you were my livery and sign. Rejoice then, for monster trucks have conquered the stadium! Rejoice for I am endless in a garter belt and slip, rejoice! For old names, for run-down voices.

I am anything living on the miniature golf course at night, crawling out onto the hushed green, unseen.

About Trace Peterson

Trace Kelsey Peterson was born in Connecticut in 1978 and has lived in Tucson, AZ, Somerville, MA and Brooklyn, NY where she currently resides. Peterson is a trans woman poet critic, the author of two books of poems and numerous chapbooks. She edits the journal/small press *EOAGH* which has won 2 Lambda Literary Awards including the first given in Transgender Poetry, and she is co-editor of the groundbreaking anthology *Troubling the Line: Trans and Genderqueer Poetry and Poetics* (Nightboat Books) as well as co-editor of *Arrive on Wave: Collected Poems of Gil Ott* (Chax Press). Her next book of poems is forthcoming from Ahsahta Press. Her poetry has recently appeared in *Readings in Contemporary Poetry: An Anthology* (Dia Art Foundation / Yale University press), *Best American Experimental Writing 2016* (Wesleyan University press), as well as *Boston Review, The Brooklyn Rail, PEN America, Posit,* and at the *Academy of American Poets* (poets.org). Her criticism and scholarly writing have appeared in *From Our Hearts to Yours: New Narrative as Contemporary Practice* (*ON Contemporary Practice,* 2017), *TSQ: Transgender Studies Quarterly,* and numerous edited collections. She has taught at Yale University, Naropa University's Summer Writing Program, The Poetry Project at St Marks, and Hunter College where she currently teaches an innovative upper-level literature course in Trans and Nonbinary Poetry.

About Chax

Founded in 1984 in Tucson, Arizona, Chax has published more than 230 books in a variety of formats, including hand printed letterpress books and chapbooks, hybrid chapbooks, book arts editions, and trade paperback editions such as the book you are holding. From August 2014 until July 2018 Chax Press resided in Victoria, Texas, where it was located in the University of Houston-Victoria Center for the Arts. UHV has supported the publication of *Since I Moved In,* which has also received support from friends of the press. Chax is a nonprofit 501(c)(3) organization which depends on support from various government private funders, and, primarily, from individual donors and readers.

In July 2018 Chax Press returned to Tucson, Arizona, while maintaining an affiliation with the University of Houston-Victoria. Our current address is 1517 North Wilmot Road no. 264, Tucson, Arizona 85712-4410. You can email us at *chaxpress@gmail.com.*

Recent books include *A Mere Rica,* by Linh Dinh, *Visible Instruments,* by Michael Kelleher, *What's the Title?,* by Serge Gavronsky, *Diesel Hand,* by Nico Vassilakis, *At Night on The Sun,* by Will Alexander, *The Hindrances of Householders,* by Jennifer Barlett, *Who Do With Words,* by Tracie Morris, *Mantis,* by David Dowker, *Rechelesse Pratticque,* by Karen Mac Cormack, *The Hero,* by Hélène Sanguinetti (transl. by Ann Cefola), *For Instance,* By Eli Goldblatt, and *Towards a Menagerie,* by David Miller.

You may find CHAX at *https://chax.org/*

A Note on the Gil Ott Memorial Book Series

The Gil Ott Memorial Book, beginning with the book you now hold and continuing as a project of Chax Press, has been established through a generous donation. The book honors the work and the legacy of poet, publisher, and social activist Gil Ott. In all of his work, Gil Ott sought forms and practices that were, as he once said in an interview, "incorruptible." His writing, in poetry and prose, searches for and finds a language that offers clarity within difficulty and without compromise, pause amid unrelenting pressure, words of love, survival, and intense honesty. As a publisher, of Singing Horse Press and the journal *Paper Air,* he presented new and unique voices, and he inspired readers everywhere. The editors for the Gil Ott Memorial book series are Charles Alexander, Eli Goldblatt, Myung Mi Kim, and Nathaniel Mackey. The task of the editors is to find individual books, first or second books by writers whose innovative practice and vision engage poetic, aesthetic, and social issues in ways that honor and extend the work of Gil Ott.